P9-DJK-192

LORD DRAGONFLY

Five Sequences

By

William Heyen

For Barbara Bash, whose True Nature has a home in me —

Edited & with an Introduction by Nate Pritts

Bill Heyen

Afterword by Matthew Henriksen

Brockport, N Y

editorial assistant: Elizabeth Brace

10/30/10

—

H_NGM_N BKS
REISSUES
www.h-ngm-nbks.com

Also by William Heyen

POETRY

Depth of Field (1970)
Noise in the Trees: Poems and a Memoir (1974)
The Swastika Poems (1977)
Long Island Light: Poems and a Memoir (1979)
The City Parables (1980)
Lord Dragonfly: Five Sequences (1981)
Erika: Poems of the Holocaust (1984)
The Chestnut Rain (1986)
Brockport, New York: Beginning with "And" (1988)
Pterodactyl Rose: Poems of Ecology (1991)
Ribbons: The Gulf War (1991)
The Host: Selected Poems 1965-1990 (1994)
Crazy Horse in Stillness (1996)
Diana, Charles, & the Queen (1998)
Shoah Train (2003)
The Rope (2003)
The Confessions of Doc Williams & Other Poems (2006)
To William Merwin: A Poem (2007)
A Poetics of Hiroshima (2008)
The Angel Voices: A Poem (2010)

PROSE

Vic Holyfield & the Class of 1957: A Romance (1986)
With Me Far Away: A Memoir (1994)
Pig Notes & Dumb Music: Prose on Poetry (1998)
The Hummingbird Corporation: Stories (2003)
Home: Autobiographies, Etc. (2004)
Titanic & Iceberg: Early Essays & Reviews (2006)
The Cabin: Journal 1964-1985 (2009)

ANTHOLOGIES

A Profile of Theodore Roethke (Ed. 1971)
American Poets in 1976 (Ed. 1976)
The Generation of 2000: Contemporary American Poets (Ed. 1984)
Dumb Beautiful Ministers: Poets from the Long Island Quarterly (Ed. 1996)
September 11, 2001: American Writers Respond (Ed. 2002)

William Heyen was born in Brooklyn, New York, in 1940, and raised in Suffolk County by German immigrant parents. His graduate degrees are from Ohio University. A former Senior Fulbright Lecturer in American Literature in Germany, he has been honored with NEA, Guggenheim, American Academy of Arts & Letters and other awards. His poetry has appeared in the Atlantic, The New Yorker, Harper's, American Poetry Review, The Southern Review, and in hundreds of other magazines and anthologies. His Crazy Horse in Stillness won the Small Press Book Award in 1997; Shoah Train: Poems was a finalist for the National Book Award in 2004. His A Poetics of Hiroshima is a 2010 selection of the Chautauqua Literary & Scientific Circle. Heyen is Professor of English/Poet in Residence Emeritus at his undergraduate alma mater, SUNY Brockport.

FIRST H_NGM_N REISSUES EDITION, JUNE 2010

Copyright © 2010 by William Heyen
Introduction © 2010 by Nate Pritts
Afterword © 2010 by Matthew Henriksen

All rights reserved. Printed in the United States of America.

ISBN 978-1-453-60800-5

Book and cover design by Scott O'Connor
Cover photograph by Susan C. Weber

For additional material on William Heyen and Lord Dragonfly, please visit:
www.h-ngm-n.com/lord-dragonfly

Editorial Acknowledgments:

Lord Dragonfly: Five Sequences was first published in 1981 (NY: Vanguard Press).

Matthew Henriksen's afterword first appeared in issue #5 of Octopus Magazine (www.octopusmagazine.com). Thanks to the editors for permission to reprint the essay here.

Author's Acknowledgements:

The Ash appeared as a chapbook from Banjo Press (Syracuse) in 1978. Thanks to Allen Hoey. "The Eternal Ash" first appeared in Skywriting, "The Ash" in Folio: Work in Progress, edited by John Slathatos and Martin Booth (London: Oxus Press/Sceptre Press, 1977). "The Zenith Ash" first appeared as an Ontario Review postcard. I've made some changes to this and the other sequences over the years that I'm glad now to get into this H_NGM_N edition.

Lord Dragonfly was first published in Poetry and subsequently in a limited edition by Scrimshaw Editions (Ruffsdale, PA) in 1978. Thanks to Ernest and Cis Stefanik. That edition included a brief afterword not reprinted in the Vanguard Press gathering, one effusively romantic, but I'm no longer an expert on the person I once was, and I've brought back that afterword here.

Abattoir Editions published Of Palestine in a limited edition in 1976. Thanks to Harry Duncan. "Papyrus," "Watermelon," "Mustard," and "Anise" first appeared in Poetry. Thanks to George Wallace at Birnham Wood Graphics (Northport, NY) who re-issued this sequence as a chapbook, with an added brief preface and dedication, in 2001.

XVII Machines was published in a limited edition by Rook Press in 1976. Some of its sections first appeared in Beloit Poetry Journal, New York Quarterly, The New York Times, Review '74, and Thistle. Several poems were reprinted in The Umbral Anthology of Science Fiction Poetry, ed. Steve Rasnic Tem (Denver, CO: Umbral Press, 1982).

Evening Dawning first appeared in a limited edition from William B. Ewert, Publisher, in 1979. The Ewert edition included a very brief prefatory note that didn't appear in the Vanguard collection. I've included it here. This sequence, and "Lord Dragonfly," were reprinted in The Host: Selected Poems 1965-1990 (St. Louis: Time Being Books, 1994).

Contents

Beginning Again:
On Reissuing William Heyen's Lord Dragonfly
by Nate Pritts

In 1992 I was a college freshman in Brockport, New York, a town where it's always fall or winter, where the Erie Canal dominates both landscape & mood, all full of bird shadows, & where sunflowers look stark & lovely against the weathered brick of academic buildings.

Seventeen & I walked up the stairs of Lathrop Hall on the SUNY Brockport campus to my first college English class & the hallway chalkboard/message center told me:

xii.

Lord Dragonfly
sees me from all sides
at once.

⁓

William Heyen's Lord Dragonfly was first published in 1981 by Vanguard Press. It went out of print at some point before the end of that decade, definitely by 1988, when their list was bought & mostly mishandled by Random House.

Rather than function as a retrospective on Heyen's career, which spans decades, continues today, & is marked most emphatically by its consistency & devotion, I'd like to focus on the book itself, my reading of it, & my friend William Heyen.

The aim of this book series, H_NGM_N Reissues, has everything to do with those traits that characterize Heyen's commitment to the art of poetry: consistency, devotion. As a reader of poetry, I yearn to have my knowledge of what it means to be human enriched by the words on the page – either through their meanings or through the way they mean. As a writer of poetry, I need to be supported in my efforts, to constantly learn, to absorb &, once saturated, to spark & flare.

It wasn't until 1993 that I first met Bill, though I had read Lord Dragonfly several times by then. I was struck immediately by his graciousness, his calm & steady exuberance. Through workshops, where he was both nurturing & fierce, & hundreds of private conversations, Bill taught me lots about poetry but even more about how to be a poet.

It is his legendary work ethic, his boundless commitment to poetry, which is Bill's biggest gift to me as a poet. It was well known around campus that Bill was up before the birds, shooting hoops with an ingrained Long Island sprezzatura that indicated it didn't matter if he made each shot though he always did. Before sunrise, he was writing poems in the Student Union, or hunkered in his office, maintaining his extraordinary journal habit or his voluminous correspondence with his own former teachers, students, brother & sister poets.

To be clear, all of this is embodied in the poetry of Lord Dragonfly, so maybe this is the place to stop talking about me, & my love, & start talking about why this book, why now.

In these poems, Heyen communicates a vision of the world as equal parts spiritual & physical. The transcendent comes together with the earthly physical again & again, resoundingly so, in a racket that is recognizably human but also luminous. It is poetry that is rooted in sensory perceptions & in the sensual – those things we can't ascertain but must simply believe.

From "Cedar" in the book's third sequence, Of Palestine:

O death
    in whose wood
        our world is tongue

we cannot hear
    and what will save us
        when will we awaken

Leaving aside a discussion of the tonal quality of this (grim

& deafening), the speaker's stance is one of ecstatic desperation. But even in these depths, bordered by death & mute wood, there is an implicit hope – not *will* we awaken, but *when*.

This transcendence, this move from crude physical thinking to a more phenomenal state of knowledge, is enacted with devastating precision. Also, it's not naïve. Some of the most powerful poems come in the book's fourth sequence, XVII Machines, where the physical isn't always pastoral or natural but instead mechanistic & brutal. How much more beautiful & ravishing, then, the transition (in "The Machine in Your Field") from a machine that "lops off your legs and arms" to this:

The machine's gentle rain will bless you.
At night its own stars will burn above you,

its moon draw blood from your bones.
You'll stretch and grow, your shoulders
will break earth. The machine will lift you,
kiss your forehead, teach you to live again.

The constant shift from delicate utterance to violent action (*bless* to *burn, draw blood* but also *lift you, kiss your forehead*) keeps the reader unbalanced but attuned, aware that "all our lives are lived / in the here and now, in one constant season" ("The Machine that Air-Conditions the World").

"Lord Dragonfly / sees me from all sides / at once." What affects me most profoundly in this collection is the visionary nature of the work, that the poems relentlessly create & enact a sense of the world as something we can know, something we must strive to know. In "The Eternal Ash," from the book's first sequence The Ash, Heyen directs the reader, in a torturous passage, to a simple goal, "yes, but to know one thing, but know it." There's an emphasis on the final "know" in that line; certainly we all agree that we can come to universal truths through knowing "one thing" but to truly "know" it – to see it from all sides at once – is something more harrowing, more fraught.

Today, with evening dawning, the landscape of contemporary poetry is littered with lines & whole poems that seek to reject this world we're stuck with, that forge a barrier between our human feelings & this emotional living we're trying to make sense of. We're having a conversation about what poetry can be & it is cluttered with ironic postures & an elaborately codified estrangement that forgets the reality it is seeking to make new. There are so many poems that forget we can be made out of words that mean, & that mean what they mean earnestly.

Lord Dragonfly is a book that challenges me in its forms of feelings, through the intricacies of its thinking, & by the linguistic deployment of both, a book sadly unavailable to a generation of readers & writers who need it. It is a book I am honored to welcome back into this ongoing conversation.

⁓

Nate Pritts is the author of three full-length books of poems - The Wonderfull Yeare (Cooper Dillon Books, 2010), Honorary Astronaut (Ghost Road Press, 2008) & Sensational Spectacular (BlazeVOX, 2007). He has his BS from SUNY Brockport ('95), his MFA in Poetry from Warren Wilson College ('00), & his PhD in British Romanticism from the University of Louisiana, Lafayette ('03). He is the founder & principal editor of H_NGM_N.

LORD DRAGONFLY: Five Sequences

Notes

Lord Dragonfly consists of five sequences of poems written between 1974 and 1979. I've arranged the sequences here not chronologically, but in an order that itself forms, it seems to me, a sequence of sequences, each a consciousness defining its crises, straining to know, coming to something it can hold to. There is a clearing in the white space between sequences, but then a circling back, if obliquely, until, I hope, Lord Dragonfly sees from all sides at once.

W.H. (1981)

Soon after its publication in 1981, Lord Dragonfly went out of print, and most copies of the paperback edition disappeared, were probably shredded, when Vanguard Press shut down and sold out to Random House. Over the years, I haven't thought much about this eccentric book of mine, but now I'm glad that it will see light again. I'm grateful to Nate Pritts of H_NGM_N BKS, and to Matthew Henriksen for his surprising essay that first appeared more than two decades after my book.

W.H. (2010)

The Ash

The Ash

"Every minute, every day,
I hate this life.
I hate the trees, I hate the sunsets,
I hate my wife."

A nurse entered the room,
handed my friend his medicine,
a cup of water and two pills,
lithium and thorazine.

Eyes glazed, sedated, but fists
clenched above his sheets:
"I hate the doctors, the meals,
the beds, these stupid illiterates

"who work here." I nodded,
saved myself, ignored him,
closed my eyes for home,
my mountain ash in white bloom

where I longed to be, ever
within its perfume-menstrual smell,
pure love mixed with pure death
mixed with pure swill

mixed with its own being
where, toward our earth's distillate,
airstreams of bees glide maddened
for blossoms of white filth.

I thought of hands dipped
into cavities of ambergris,
of tongues licking scented necks,
lips sucking pus, maggots

humming their hymn of blue flame
in a dead animal's lung,
of the rainbow glaze of mucus,
the milky beauty of pond-scum,

of my own oval of flowering ash
in evening air, those powers that sustain
my body's sick-room odors,
the twisted smiles, the sunlit skin

cancers, the hate-vapors drifting
toward my broken friend who cried
"I hate books, I hate the seasons,
I hate children, I hate the dead."

Where, if ever, will this end?
My friend moves from one ward to another,
embedded, circling lower. For now, outside,
I circle closer to the white ash flower.

The Ash: Its End

June, and gone is the flowering ash's
too-full menstrual odor,
with which I lived. Only thin perfume
lingers on the air

after its earthly love where white
blossoms have rusted:
tree at the end of something, almost
pure spirit at its end.

The Eternal Ash

By early August, the tree's each limb
hangs heavy, its berry clusters
already tinged orange and bending its body
almost to breaking. The ash bears,

and will, this light, this weight.
Even at night under the frost stars, each berry
deepens into the ripe flame
autumn means for it to be,

yes, but to know one thing, but know it:
the lord of the whole tree, in time,
unchanged, its changes mine, delusion;
knowing, now, the mystical winter blossom....

Which August is this, anyway?— this windless
poise of clusters that never fall, but will,
within the living tree that withers, while
ashlight drifts to the earth, petal by petal

The Flowering Mountain Ash Berry

Sperm floating in air,
   the earth to be its bed,
      packed in wet orange flesh,
         one luminous oval seed.

The Zenith Ash

September winds are elsewhere, have missed her.
Now the green oval of the flowering ash flames.
If I do not take her now,
while berry-clusters hemorrhage her limbs ...

She is the holiness begun with one seed,
Yours, my Lord. Your
summer has burnished her branches
to this brown-black shine. Her

body does not wait. Time
is. If I, in human error, lose her,
even You, my Lord, will curse me:
each seed in each berry a skull's leer.

Now the green oval of the flowering tree
flames. And You are the slanting cancerous rays
of autumn sunlight, and You
the source that takes me, and this my ash of praise.

The Friend

Winter. My friend is not my friend,
probably will not return, raves and drools
oblivious to me, the doctors, the walls,
stares into a labyrinth's dead end

where history and logic die:
"I hate the chairs, the words,
the winds, the bastards
in bed with me all night."

But this time, home again
from visiting him, I stepped
from my car onto the shocked bone
of my body, and walked

into the snow-sheathed tree. No gloves
to touch it, I touched it, caressed it.
Flesh burned into its silhouette,
froze: held fast, I wept in waves until

the tree flared, ice-white as stars:
You, Lord, saw, had left me to see,
to say goodbye to my dead friend,
and to love the dead.

Lord Dragonfly

i.

A friend dies.
Another,
forcing the lilac to flower.

ii.

In a corner of the field, wild
grapevine climbs a lightning
groove in the ash trunk.
Where are the dead?

iii.

In the field's drizzle and gloom,
soft-glowing sheaths,
the souls of spikes
of goldenrod.

iv.

Breaking the field I find
a ring of round white stones,
gift of the glacier.

v.

As I dig, the old apple stump
tries pulling itself deeper
by its last root.

vi.

Inside the windfall apple
tunnels of bees
singing.

vii.

I'm glad,
grasshopper of my childhood,
you've grown your legs back.

viii.

Pure white found
a wild rose to live in,
for now.

ix.

Half the mantis still
prays on my scythe blade.

x.

In the mowed field,
a million crickets for hire.
My steps are money.

xi.

My wife away.
In a garden furrow,
I find her lost earring.

xii.

Lord Dragonfly
sees me from all sides
at once.

xiii.

Pear blossoms
sift the same air
as last year.

xiv.

No one has ever
seen snow fall here,
until next year.

xv.

The hummingbird whirrs,
only its ruby
throat feathers clear.

xvi.

Curves of the summer pepper
lit with every green.

xvii.

With trees overhead
where is the void?

xviii.

One red cardinal,
one gray cardinal,
three cinnamon-spotted eggs.

xix.

I am safe here,
not a friend in sight.

xx.

I lean on my shovel,
trusting the field.

xxi.

Playing dead,
Japanese beetles tumble
from a skeleton leaf.

xxii.

Already morning glory
tendrils circle
my shovel's handle.

xxiii.

Beneath its tassels
an ear of corn
erupts in fungus,
the blackest light.

xxiv.

When I look for him,
he is away,
finding another home,
the borer that killed my poplar.

xxv.

Prune for shade.

xxvi.

Rooted,
the trees are green islands
in fog
in the shifting field.

xxvii.

Sunflower, my lamp,
on such a rainy day.

xxviii.

Tree-man
carrying branches
of silver maple
I walk through the storm.

xxix.

Evening: time to level
the frantic anthill,
the field's brain.

xxx.

Meteor shower—
a little more, or less,
of the Lord.

xxxi.

Outside at night
I close my eyes:
the lost chestnuts' roots
luminous underground.

xxxii.

This western corner of the field,
this grove of ash—
if there were a place ...

xxxiii.

Beetle's cargo:
heaviness?
happiness?
Neither, nor
both together.

xxxiv.

In the far galaxies,
collapsed stars,
yes, but here,
light escapes
even the blackberries.

xxxv.

In the autumn field,
my body,
a warm stone.

xxxvi.

Cosmos, planet, field,
and the dead
aware of everything!

For ten years I've lived in Brockport in western New York State on a street of middle-class homes, four hundred miles and about three decades from the Long Island of woods and ponds and farms I knew as a child. But I've come to love this village, and doubt that I'll ever leave it for long, except to return to the source. Even then, I will be here.

Once or twice each autumn, on the roof of my house to clean gutters, I've looked south past the Erie Canal to the white bell tower of Hartwell Hall at the college where I teach, about a mile away. I've been too involved with my "career," and it was only a couple of years ago, as I looked out over Brockport, that I realized that the only un-developed land left backed my own quarter-acre plot. My back lawn ended in a dense wall of apple brush, and trees, and briers.

The proverbial distant old woman really did own this land, and rumors floated around that it was in the process of being sold to a contractor and subdivided. I expected this, and was complacent about it, until I began walking the land and seeing what could be lost.

Somehow, after tricky negotiations with the woman's lawyer, a neighbor managed to buy the land, and last year my wife and I managed to buy an acre of the three from him. I was nervous while the papers were going through.

Only an acre, but an acre, half a lawn/meadow/garden and half of trees that will keep apartment houses at bay for at least the rest of my life, is a very big place. I feel free back there, digging and planting or standing still, as I've never in my adult life felt before. In one of his poems the twentieth-century Japanese master Ippekiro, translated by Soichi Furuta, says

Neither life nor death

seems to be there
magnolia in bloom

and it is this dimension I so often enter when I walk back there to work and discover. At these times, even when I hide myself among the trees, I hold memories of cities within me, airports, bus stations. When in the cities, of course, I will bear this land, my past made present again, but more.

One acre. The geologic history of the continent bends in to me here, and the particular human history of this canal village. I'll never be able to say what it meant for me to clear brush from around three silver maples, to find raspberry bushes, to find three catalpas and two horse-chestnut saplings, to walk with my wife into a blooming patch of her favorite wild flower, Black-eyed Susan.

And my own history: gulls sweep by ranging out from Lake Ontario, a dozen miles north, as gulls flew over Nesconset when I was a boy. I can hear, too, the bells of two canal bridges. From this far, I swear, the bells make the same clanking sound as those bells on Wenzel's cows, coming home.

I found the poems of Lord Dragonfly over several weeks during the summer of 1977. There were many more, but these, now a sequence, seem best to me to light up from within and stay lit under their own power as, beginning in darkness, they move into the profusion of their blessed field.

(1978)

Of Palestine

I've never visited the Holy Lands, but tried to imagine them and their misery and beauty by way of this quiet group of poems, a meditation. My theme here (as heard decades after I wrote this sequence) seems to be "the world's sorrow never grown old," the region's ubiquitous and eternally ramifying grief. The poems do not take sides here, I hope; their speaker, in fact, seems to reveal in "Flax" what might be his own central and undercutting question that points up for him the tragic irony of religious bloodshed.

I'd like to dedicate these poems to the memory of the extraordinary artist Alfred Van Loen.

W.H.
(December 2000)

Almond

Palestine turns again to the year's first days.
Now, the almond bursts its head
into white and airy blossom.

What is this speech spoken in the wind,
in the bloom of the almond's white air?
What should we know of the blood's winter?

Old Arab, old Jew, or tree that you are,
snow-white January almond,
we can almost hear.

Papyrus

Once abundant, now rare,
growing almost in water, or in water,
its pith cut into strips and layered,
it was this that held the words.

Triangular stem, slender
leaves tufting ten feet above the marsh,
it was this that held the words,
the words of sunlight, or words

spoken, or breathed, or dreamed,
or gotten down on it with reed pens,
with soot and gum-thickened water.
It was papyrus held the words.

We could listen as it swayed in wind
above the sounds of water,
speaking with words of water,
words of sunlight in its leaves.

Lily of the Field

Consider them, said Jesus,
how they grow
and do not toil, nor spin.
But even Solomon,
in all his glory,
was not arrayed like one.

We have seen them in their lids
of scarlet-red; but sometimes
white in Galilee, or on
the Plain of Sharon; but sometimes
Jaffa fields blow pale
blue with their delicate lashes.

Stem of tiny nerves
braided, six petals
Solomon's royal color,
and pupil of black seeds—
all pressed here
into our book as its eye.

Madonna Flower

No scripture names it.
The name for it came later.
Still, she would have seen it,
Mary, the mother its name remembers.
She would have seen it,
in Nazareth, and known it,
as other mothers, Arab and Jew,
still know it,

its white petals and feathery leaves—
we will place it
in clay bowls for their tables,
or on the fresh graves
of their children, or, when time weaves,
as it will, again, as it has,
over their abdomens that swell,
under their hearts that grieve.

Passion Everlasting

Palestine remembers.
They were tipped red before.
And such a deep red suddenly to issue
from stems gray-white as ghosts.

They were tipped red before:
the flowing bodies of believers, disbelievers.
They have held buds of blood
above the ground as though the whole earth

were straining to bear the young men up
as do the weeping women
of so many paintings. Palestine
remembers: flowers for all passions everlasting.

Pheasant's Eye

Or called Adonis,
another flower to remember losses,
drops of blood. That handsome lad
is dead. In Palestine, innocent
eyes shine and weep
red droplets to the grasses.
Next spring, Adonis blooms again.

Watermelon

The dry soil itself,
the sandy soil itself—
this is the temple, this
the miraculous dark mosque
of the melon placed
in Palestine for our tongues
to taste, to which we listen:

O Lords, your vines
are the melon's springs and rivers.
Allah, Jehovah,
what speech is this?
what words are these
that pulse fruit
from among the leaves, these

vowels intoning
low sounds in the wind, these
hard-skinned tear-
shaped melons, these
dusty gourds our thumbs
touch to glistening
greens and yellows?

Bean

Kneel with us, now,
within the ruins the Arabs call Chartula,
a hilltop where Joshua
commanded the sun and moon: *Stand still!*

Look down with us, now,
through the pass through the mountains
through the sacred land:
O Jerusalem.

The plant we will taste is tender,
but has survived,
leaves and tendrils multitudinous
as Allah's eyes,

its blossoms yellow
with a few dark stripes,
the Jew's star,
or his coat.

There is not yet
an ending to this.
The truth harbors
the bean's vine twisting

into thick matting
above the rich soil of ruins.
Allah, Jehovah, we taste
bitter love but pray for peace.

Mustard

Down at the lake we looked about us,
saw tares growing among the wheat,
saw fishermen at their nets,
saw the mustard's yellow blossoms,
pods bursting at the ends of stiff stems.

In dry graves its seeds have passed
millennia like minutes. Brought to light again,
these sprout in new tears. Tares, wheat,
fishermen still at their nets
under the golden sun, and mustard, for us

to taste the world's sorrow never grown old,
wisdom powdered to bloom on the tongue.

Cyclamen

Cyclamen aleppicum,
one of spring's first flowers,
unaware of its own Latin, so common is it,
so little does it need a name
to lisp its own sweetness to the air,

needing only mountains,
only its own blossoms of several colors
from pure white to spotted lavenders,
only the water its roots can kiss,
and April's gentle beginning flames.

Flax

In Egypt, in Palestine, flax
woven to linen wrapped
the dead.

Beige, cream, brown, white linen, but
nothing of the lavender flax
blossom that lights

whole hills in the living distance, not a word
of the slightest mauve speaks
from the linen,

and if death is as colorless as this, if
the Bible is wrong and the Koran
wrong and the Talmud

wrong that say those judged when that day
patterns the woof and warp, those
"companions of the right hand"

shall live forever with their Lord—
if the holy writings
are wrong,

if it is true that death is the beige, cream,
brown, white weave of flax,
if this is true ...

Cedar

To lie down
  to sleep in the last grove
    of these oldest mothers

to breathe the resinous
  balsamic odors
    leaf and bole

to dream to fall
  from time to die
    to lose yourself

under evergreen air
  bark your pillow
    roots your hair

above you the earth's
  slight curve the trees'
    conical heads the sky's

blue-black dome
  how have you fallen
    this far

O death
  in whose wood
    our world is tongue

we cannot hear
  and what will save us
    when will we awaken

Lentil

What is the lentil's propaganda?
Which is its flag?

For beauty, for speech:
its pink tongues.

What is its passion?
Whose holy books burn
blood-red behind its million eyes?

For constant miracle, the lentil takes
to poorest soil, yields
fragrant pottage.

As the cities die,
and the people die?...

For the end of the world,
for after the end, the lentil.

Palm

One:
one
hundred
feet high:
taller than
idols, and alive,
wide leaves waving
over its knotted
trunk,
dates
in fifteen-
pound
clusters,
fruit
whose stones
we feed
to camels,
or mash for human
medicine.
We cut the tree
for baskets,
bags,
mats,
brushes;
for fences,
poultry
cages;
for thread,
ropes,
rigging;
for sap
liquor;
for thatch
shelter;
for fuel;

for wreaths
of honor;
for cover
for corpses;
for images
of conduct
in the wind,
tree never
aspiring
to heaven,
living
itself
in its own heaven
as the planet
circles,
as the galaxy
drifts
to nowhere we
will ever know,
this vertical
numinous
whip, this
shapeshifting
shade, this
palm
rooted
one
hundred
feet
deep
in our only
holiness,
soul,
earth's
sand,
soil,
rock.

Grass

"All flesh is as grass," said Peter,
    "but the word of the Lord endureth." ...
We have pressed wordless grasses into pages.
    Our flesh is in the grasses.

Anise

These are the last words of this, our prayer
to enter the anise yellow as sunlight,

to sleep in the shade
of the fig's five-lobed leaves,

in the calm of the cedar's horizontal branches,
to be dazed into rest by the mandrake's

magical human root, to dream
in medicinal anise light,

in the light of the leek's
invisible distillate,

of this land, this power, this
bulb, this Palestine broken open

under eyes that film with it,
and fill with tears.

XVII Machines

Machines To Kiss You Goodnight

Under the world's mountains
fossils tell the old story:
coal flowers shine
in their own black light.

Machines, rooted in bedrock,
question and answer themselves, recall
their dreams of numbers,
the sweet possibilities of fire.

Rockets hiss as though praying
for release, for the long arc under the sun,
then to tongue the earth again,
to kiss you, to flame.

The Machine That Kills Cats

In an advanced technological society
the licensing of machinery
is the sole province of the state,
forever inviolate,

except for the patriotic few eccentric
sometimes angry inventive mechanics
and scientists whose daily food
is also the bread of the common good,

and therefore I have sailed the seas
in full knowledge to please
those like myself who favor rats
and birds, and hate cats.

As a first gift to men
I built my machine
to hound them in their dark alleys,
or among vines and lilies,

where it clamps its iron jaws
on their backs, claws
their green eyes out with steel wires,
and sets them afire

until they burn to black dust.
My machine is the first
of many such whose one thought
is to track and kill the cat.

The Machine That Collects Butterflies

Today is a lepidopterist's delight:
monarchs, swallowtails, rare finchwings
flutter and gambol in the meadow like lambs;
zephyrs bend the long grasses to waves.

Moving on a soft rush of air,
following your eye that follows
the single elusive butterfly
you've been searching for for so long,

the machine whispers a fine spray
that rainbows in the gold light,
brings your prize down to your feet
like a leaf: dead, beautiful,

and perfect, even the dust on its wings
shining for years in your glass box.

The Master

Chess is not poetry, chess
is mathematics to the nth.
Track the master to his fifth move.
He'll track you to your tenth.

The steel trap of his mind:
sixty-four squares to shut upon.
This is the prose of iron,
not the poetry of winds,

fluids, curves, breaks, bends,
accidents or passions.
His moves are instant.
Your game ends

on a feudal rack
black and painful as the plague:
his queen, the spider of her several corridors,
and yours; his bishops,

the sole power of their diagonals;
his knights at your throat
with the jagged L's
of their axes. And as you die,

because his world was never
in doubt, never more secure,
his king sleeps a dreamless sleep
behind the stone towers of the royal bower.

The Line

The belt, a metal river, runs
its mile-long gauntlet of machines
bending above it like its mother,
goddess of hammers and shears.

O, lovely mother
of aluminum and oil,
mane of levers
and eyes of wheel,

fingers of knives
and kiss of laser,
breath of fume,
embrace of wire,

build slowly while I sing this song.
Because our lives are flesh, and short.
Because your art is longer, your
boys of piston, girls of gear.

The Machine That Mends Birds' Nests

It's on its own, dispossessed,
day and night treads streets,
fields, corridors of buildings,
and the deep woods.

For somewhere a loose shoelace
threatens a child, a beam rots,
broken bottles need sweeping,
ice cracks a sidewalk, a cat

cries from a closet, ivy chokes
saplings, or a circuit shorts.
It's on its own now, its metal heart
obsessed with perfection.

A nest endangers its eggs:
even the oblivious robins blink
as this machine reaches up to bend
a twig here, to replace a grassblade, there.

The Machine That Air-Conditions The World

The Congo's hippo, the Nile's
cloudy myth-of-a-blue riverhorse who
all day chewed his cud
of lily-pads, who
all day drowsed in mud,
dreaming of flight while birds
pecked and danced his head,
now tiptoes
and cavorts the brush,
his whole being fluttering like flamingos.
On occasion, even Libya snows.

Now that the earth's one
air-conditioned hippodrome,
now that M.I.T.'s machine
monitors the world and beams
its cool breath over to Boston
or across the oceans,
now that the deserts' hot winds
and sandstorms are only the Bedouins'
old tales or, once in a while, someone's
sweaty dream, all our lives are lived
in the here and now, in one constant season.

The Machine That Treats Other Machines

This one, the most human,
can kill, has hands
that can crush gears, tubes,
tapes, parts beyond redemption.

This one is sure of itself as God.
When it destroys, it destroys;
when it repairs, its long and triple-
jointed touch is deft as a surgeon's.

Another machine sleeps at its switch:
this one embraces its ill brother,
dismantles, or cures. Impossible,
but no man told or tells it which.

One Machine's Perversity

It could never get things right.
No means of machinations
could straighten it out.
Drank its instructions

like booze, sliced saplings in half
but spared the vines that choked them,
watered thistles and yanked roses,
mowed fields of green corn,

sprayed houseplants with oily urine,
killed, so to speak, the hounds,
and fed the rabid fox, an ox
lumbering clumsy the world's china shop.

When, at last, history's greatest lemon
ran down, we placed it in a zoo,
behind glass. Science is still lost
to know what told it what to do.

The Machine That Balances Your Mood

Your guts tighten,
your brainwaves say
murder:
the machine's sensors
pulse, its face-plate
cracks a metal smile
like a damned fool,
a rusty comedian,
a mess of comic bolts, until
your red mood passes.

Or you say,
the hell with it all
and rush toward hell,
drain a bottle
of bad wine
by nine in the morning:
the machine steps up,
a Prussian officer,
shouts for order, becomes
your new drummer.

Or you're so
unreasonably happy
you can bless death
and wish to die:
the machine
clanks up,
moves to an oil and whirr
of tragic arrangement,
restores you
to a luke-warm world.

Now, at night,
as you walk from steady
shadows of trees held steady
in the steady
air, cricketsong
twirps along your nerves,
small acceptable scrapes,
while each star completes the scene,
ganglia and neuron,
of a friendly constellation.

The Companion Machine

It toasts and butters,
watches you scan the morning papers, asks:
What do you think of those damned Chinese?
Did you see the report on the blue robins?

Your answers etched on its inner ears,
it nods, checks the barometer back of its head,
gathers your hat, umbrella and rubbers,
washes the dishes and makes your bed,

tells you how well you look today, o-
pens your door and walks you out: O
smell the rainy air today,
and wipe your rainy eyes, O

and kiss your machine goodbye today,
and kiss your machine goodbye. O.

The Machine As Jewish Mother

She knows you're tired, hungry,
down to your last few coins.
She murmurs and prepares.

Her eyes light up. Her breath
steams like a cup of soup.
You whisper thanks and drink

the broth of her breasts, and chew
bits of chicken,
whole again, beyond confusion.

The Machine That Kisses You Goodnight

It runs on oil scented to pine.
Its shadow is a canopy of leaves.
Its gears mesh like grass.
It does not streak linen with grease.

It stands by your bed, a tree
of lights glowing soft as orchids
in the dark. It purrs and whispers
sleep, my pretty one, sleep.

After it reaches down, like the rain,
to kiss you, you'll dream all night:
bending above you, your metal mother
keeps you from harm. Sleep. Dream.

The Wedding

After its great hands have held
the two of you in the one chapel
of its cupped palms
for a time you've lost all track of—

after the soundless music
of your loved one's love
has reached you
deeper than hearing—

after each of you is placed lost
and alone in the far valleys
of dark and are found again
to die together in satin—

after you break fast
with wine and flowers
and the words are told you
from the beginning—

you will walk out.
You will kneel in the shadow of its arms.
You will give thanks.
You will know you are wed.

The Machine In Your Field

Its fingers caress your chest
and reach in, pull out your heart.
And so on—liver, kidneys, teeth, lungs,
anything old, or diseased.

It lops off your legs and arms,
lifts your trunk, a cutting,
above the rich loam.
It plants you, heaps earth

in a mound around your neck.
You'll dry and dream in its rays.
The machine's gentle rain will bless you.
At night its own stars will burn above you,

its moon draw blood from your bones.
You'll stretch and grow, your shoulders
will break earth. The machine will lift you,
kiss your forehead, teach you to live again.

This Hydraulic

This hydraulic lifts
your dark lungs and soul
toward the sun
in a glass bubble, a cell
of ease and sweet scents
that will never burst.

This hydraulic's steel shaft
bends in the wind
like a long-stemmed rose.
This hydraulic sways,
in a mild and lemon light,
above the clouds.

You'll sleep and dream, sun-
light will flower your bed of wires
to a tangle of tendrils,
until you'll awaken,
again a child, again
and again a child.

The Machine That Puts You To Sleep

There does come a time,
after your several new lives,
to die. Your soul knows when,
and tells you, sometimes trembles
under a warm sun,
sometimes warms your limbs and face
in a flurry of snow
as though your bones were candles.
You know, and by this time
welcome your own soul's choice.
Those around you,
all those you've loved
for so long, will watch your eyes
begin to bloom to black flowers,
and will know, and be happy,
looking ahead to their own time.

Your soul will tell you the morning.
Your loved ones will walk you
to the machine's door, say
a few words, and walk away.
You'll enter the machine,
walk in the dark to where
a wall of water glows
with its own black light.
You'll walk into the water.
Your lungs will breathe water.
The water will lift you to where
your lives will pass before you
like a film. Now the machine's tides
will turn in deep silence. Now,
as though the moon drew you,
downward, the machine will drop you,
at last, into your dreamless sleep.

Evening Dawning

i.

A crow's black squawk—
my white field lost again.

ii.

All bone,
feet numb,
rhythm gone,
I clod across the field.

iii.

From the outer world,
a siren, and a dog's
painsong.

iv.

In high snow,
which way the root,
which way the tip
of the bramble arch?

v.

Sparrow hearts
criss-crossing
the frozen field.

vi.

In the long, lowest needles
of white pine,
a message,
frozen in urine.

vii.

White moon shell,
and a single gull
flying toward me
from shore.

viii.

Upswirl, sudden
white-out.
My cabin within,
I close my eyes to find it.

ix.

My footprints already
in front of me,
I walk toward the other world.

x.

Bowing,
I address the door,
pray, once more,
for that opening
to everywhere,
and enter.

xi.

Pine chair cold,
hands cold,
mind cold
and ready.

xii.

World, mind, words—
wax, wick, matches.

xiii.

Under my cabin,
field mice,
and China.

xiv.

To see the white sea,
I and my old pen knife
scrape a porthole
in the frosted window.

xv.

Rabbit tracks,
rabbit pellets,
my own footsteps
drifting with snow.

xvi.

What kind of blood
in the red-twig dogwood?

xvii.

They disappear,
St. Francis now a spruce
receiving sparrows
into his dark boughs.

xviii.

Logic, logic—
trillions of intricate hexagons.

xix.

From another time
at field's edge
the first ash
veiled in a dream
in falling snow.

xx.

Cardinal,
mote of male blood
in the winter ash.

xxi.

Under the snow,
infinitesimal pearls,
insects speeding
to summer.

xxii.

Already ferns
frost my window.

xxiii.

I am thirty-eight.
Evening is dawning.

xxiv.

Lord, winter,
I place this cabin
in your begging bowl.

xxv.

Dying, the brain
sheds cells.
In the end,
perfect numbers,
the mind,
the Milky Way's stars.

xxvi.

Candlebeam and dust,
river and fish,
as long as they last.

xxvii.

Blue stars in the blue snow
over the elm stump.

xxviii.

In the window,
holding out their pale arms,
my mother and father,
above, within, beyond the field.

xxix.

I have come to have
everything, but now
the miserable
weep in chapels
under the spruce boughs

xxx.

Even winter evenings
spore of black knot, killer
of cherry, plum, and apple,

xxxi.

mindless, invisible,
drift over the field,
but will anchor.

xxxii.

Verdun, Belsen, Jonestown—still,
from indwelling darkness, human
music, a summons
to praise.

xxxiii.

A boy, I killed these sparrows
whose *tsweet, tsweet* now
enters my cabin,
forgiving everything.

xxxiv.

I still hear
the summer woodpecker, red
godhead hammering holes
into my heartwood.

xxxv.

How long have I been here,
scent of pinesap
flowing through my chair?

xxxvi.

Snow clouds,
Milky Way nowhere in sight,
moon hidden, all
earth gone—
there is a life, this one,
beyond the body.

When the Perceiver is Priest:
Appreciation of William Heyen's Lord Dragonfly
by Matthew Henriksen

Smoky with knowledge, *Lord Dragonfly: Five Sequences* teaches the intimacy of accessibility. All master poets offer profound music, but Heyen has trimmed his lines so thoroughly they ring a primary simplicity. Like a fusion of Whitman's natural observation and the clarity of Oriental introspection, the poems so emphatically adhere to their images, both visual and visionary, that they approach objective emotionality. A force that is not Heyen's courses through these poems as he steps back, honest to experience and devoted to allowing the experience to coincide unaltered with its artifice.

The five sequences form around an ambiguous, pervasive center, "each a consciousness defining its crises, straining to know, coming to something it can hold to," Heyen announces in a brief prefatory note. Each sequence as it is read seems to become a center for the others, then rejoins the outer circle when the white space reappears. The five conceits, each true to a thematic constraint and their formal elements, seek to disclose an unnamable presence that is at once the apparent source of vitality and sorrow.

The first sequence, "The Ash," charts the mourner's cathartic restraint toward a dying friend by immersing grief into the idea of his mountain ash, an incredibly subtle, mostly narrative rendering of the deep image, though in Heyen's poems the image is overcome by the word that conceives it. The title poem, which conjures literally the ash tree while suggesting invasively many figurative degenerative ashes, describes visits to a dying friend, descending into madness, with oblique tenderness and a spiritual lashing at self,

> I nodded,
> but tried to save myself, ignored him,
> closed my eyes, thought (for this was May)
> of my mountain ash in white bloom[.]

Confronted with his friend's death and dispersion of intellect while absorbed in his own life, he recognizes the essential guilt of the living, manifest in the "ash," "pure love mixed with pure death/mixed with pure swill/mixed with its own being," the substance of which he sees growing from cycles of existence and decomposition and calls them, "blossoms of white filth." For his intellect to resist descent into dejection and horror by over-empathizing with his friend, Heyen concedes a necessary, nearly sinister detachment

> of my own oval of flowering ash
> in evening air, those powers that sustain
> my body's sick room odors,
> the twisted smiles, the sunlit skin
>
> cancers, the hate-vapors drifting
> toward my broken friend[.]

The sequence continues by meditating on the tree passing through seasons, not something to doubt Heyen's getting away with, because these are masterful, purposeful, and of timeless quality. Heyen understands the Oriental nature poem deeply enough to adopt the techniques of voluminous imagery and immaculate detachment to the poetic traditions of the rural Northeast and of the style of his own time. The poems so thoughtfully invert their images (of the tree) into thought ("The ash bears,/and will, this light, this weight") that we forget the dying friend until the concluding poem of the sequence. "The Friend" begins flatly, "Winter. My friend is not my friend," and describes a last visit to the hospital, admitting all the sentimentalities of grief from which the speaker had earlier detached, and ending with a farewell spoken to God and the tree. In a manner similar in different ways to Rilke's and Whitman's, Heyen takes us to the place where intellectual restraint admits its ultimate failure and revives itself only through grief, best done in the face of beauty.

The second sequence, "Lord Dragonfly," explores nature through Haiku-like, image-centered meditations. Early on, the poems continue the theme of "The Ash":

> In a corner of the field, wild
> grapevine climbs a lightning
> groove in the ash trunk.
> Where are the dead?

The poems gradually become more personal, abstracting the confrontation with death to a conflict between perception and nature. Denser and trickier than the more obviously formal "The Ash," "Lord Dragonfly" finds hidden music both in nature and the line: "Breaking the field I find/a ring of round white stones,/gift of the glacier." The sequence, like "The Ash," moves toward the abstract as the imagery is internalized ("With trees overhead,/Where is the void?"), finally introducing the visionary ("Outside at night/I close my eyes:/the lost chestnuts' roots/luminous underground."), and, in the last poems, expanding into the cosmos in a transcendental send up. And why not? Out of grief, we rise, and through artifice, we exalt. When the perceiver is priest, the body becomes altar to nature. How literally must we take Emerson, Whitman, and Heyen? Isn't the religious experience as literal as the mathematical? And if so, what does the form of it matter?

Heyen's poems lead toward such questions because of their accessibility and clarity, which doesn't necessitate good poems but does allow, as also in the case of James Wright, a sublime contrast of detachment. In our tradition, poets who indulge in language seem often more immersed in subject (think Hopkins, as opposed to Browning; Hart Crane, as opposed to John Crowe Ransom). As Heyen continues in the third section, "Of Palestine," to describe the sensory experiences, medicinal properties, and historical and symbolic significances of Biblical flowers, we find a synthesis of immersion in subject and emotional detachment. Heyen doesn't, as Zukofsky does in 80 Flowers, make his poems into representations of flowers, but instead lets his voice present his complete perception of the flowers. The brilliance of this method in this centrally located sequence is that while flowers strike all the senses but sound, through their traditions and, ultimately, their names, the flowers evoke sound in the intellect. A strong example occurs at the opening of "Madonna Flower":

> No scripture names it.
> The Name for it came later.
> Still, she would have seen it,
> Mary, the mother its name remembers.

Each poem in the sequence attempts to remember the sensual existences of past people through the flowers, immune to conflict and decay, finally likening, by way of the words of Peter ("All flesh is as grass, but the word of the Lord endureth"), human permanence through a reflective conceit.

"XVII Machines," more fanciful, ironic, and far less emotive than the other sequences, enumerates a menagerie of imaginary machines that seem to exist in a world beyond cathartic indulgences. In "The Machine That Collects Butterflies," the day "is a lepidopterist's delight," a mechanical misconstruing, in the absence of the lepidopterist, of her love for life as a love for destroying life:

> the machine whispers a fine spray
> that rainbows in the golden light,
> brings your prize down to your feet
> like a leaf: dead, beautiful,

> and perfect[.]

Where the other sequences move toward meditation, "XVII Machines" faces the subject through observation, as in "The Machine That Treats Other Machines," ("This one, the most human, can kill") and proverbial, as in "One Machine's Perversity," ("Science is still lost/to know what told it what to do"). Heyen finds his way through the disaster by confronting death as oblivion through our power to live with its impending possibility. Even destroying ourselves by over-mechanization is, in a certain sense, a human act that cannot undo the beauty of a life that is any way temporal.

The final sequence, "Evening Dawning," returns to the Haiku-like form, though these poems are less nature-oriented and more concerned with their verbal reactions to nature, less concerned with death and more with the functions and limitations of perception: "A crow's black squawk—/my white field lost again." Though these poems aren't supposed to conventionally "end" the revolving sequence, they bring the sequences to one possible epitome, where language contains meaning through a Keatsian synthesis with object. "Sparrow hearts/criss-crossing/the frozen field" is complete neither as representation or imagistic meditation, but the musical coinciding of emotion and vision captures the intention of the sequences: to dance in and out of mind through sensory and emotional faculties, not just for want of diversion, but to purposefully seek a similarity of perspective through as many faculties as it can, like the eyes of "Lord Dragonfly," which "sees me from all sides at once." While Heyen walks back and forth from cabin to wood, he finds the "other world" of mind-and-object. The world is sustained by metaphor as literal and the negotiable durance of time. The sequence also remembers "The Ash" through a distorted perspective:

> From another time
> at field's edge
> the first ash
> veiled in a dream
> in falling snow.

Then Heyen envisions the dispersion of his intellect, though not of self perceived as part of the cosmic mind:

Dying, the brain
sheds cells.
In the end,
perfect numbers,
the mind,
the Milky Way's stars.

The grief of the early poems still resides in the speaker's voice, but a
cosmic grace akin to oblivion or loss of memory presides:

A boy, I killed these sparrows
whose *tsweet, tsweet* now
enters my cabin,
forgiving everything.

Lord Dragonfly: Five Sequences makes as strong a case as any
long poem since Roethke's "North American Sequence" that through
natural observation and introspective clarity the intellect discovers
itself as non-physical and non-temporal, a part of an abstract life
"beyond the body" immediately available to us. Heyen's style is so
in tune with the traditions of the American nature poem, the New
England Transcendentalist, and the Oriental mystic that he seems
to say the ancient abstract in its most specific terms, while putting
newness behind it through a personal vocabulary of deep imagery
becoming pure language—a move that seems to have predicted the
direction many young poets are taking today.

Matthew Henriksen lives and teaches in the Ozark
Mountains. With his wife, Katy Henriksen, he publishes Cannibal
Books, a literary book arts press. He also co-edits the online poetry
magazine Typo. His first full-length collection of poems, *Ordinary
Sun*, will emerge from Black Ocean in 2011.

H_NGM_N BKS Reissues seek to honor the individual volume as the ultimate realization of a writer's vision, republishing out of print or scarce volumes judged to be essential to our contemporary conversations of poetics/aesthetics.

www.h-ngm-n.com
www.h-ngm-nbks.com

5656095R0

Made in the USA
Charleston, SC
16 July 2010